THE HOOD

THE HOOD

Journal of Poetic Justice for the Next Generation

RANDALL D.E. BEVERLY

J. Merrill
PUBLISHING

ISBN: 978-1-950719-47-1 (Paperback)
ISBN: 978-1-950719-48-8 (eBook)

Library of Congress Control Number: 2020915708

Any references to historical events, real people, or real places are used fictitiously. Names, characters, and places are products of the author's imagination.

FIRST printing edition 2020.

J Merrill Publishing, Inc.
434 Hillpine Drive
Columbus, OH 43207

www.JMerrillPublishingInc.com

Beautiful Wife

Your internal and external beauty is proof that heaven exists and represents the truth of an eternal blessing that will be loved, honored, cherished, respected, and celebrated for as long as I live.

Beautiful Children

You are all, indeed, the best gifts I could have ever received from a creator who has entrusted your mother and I with the opportunity to raise as well as watch you grow and develop into awesome and powerful human beings. If the world was a dollar bill looking for change, I hope and pray that you will be the four quarters that help facilitate that change for generations to come.

CONTENTS

PURPOSE

To poetically broaden the definition of a word in the form of a letter that allows the reader to navigate through hoods people encounter in life. The reader is further invited to ponder information as well as express thoughts and feelings by answering questions related to the topic of each poem. Life on earth is temporal, but the impact one can have on a life is eternal. I hope the next generation will light and spark an eternal flame of positivity that will never be extinguished.

HOOD

by Randall D.E. Beverly

A TERM USED LOOSELY AND CULTURALLY SCARY,
YET BROAD IS THE WORD FOUND IN A DICTIONARY.

: A LOOSE PLIABLE COVERING FOR THE HEAD AND NECK,
EITHER ATTACHED TO A ROBE, A JACKET, OR SEPARATE

: AN ORNAMENTAL CLOTH HUNG FROM THE SHOULDERS OF AN ACADEMIC
OR ECCLESIASTICAL ROBE

: A SACK USED TO COVER A FALCON'S HEAD TO KEEP IT QUIET
: SOMETHING RESEMBLING A HOOD- IN SHAPE OR IN FUNCTION
: A METAL COVER OR COWL OVER A STOVE, A CARRIAGE TOP, OR HINGED
METAL LID OVER AN AUTOMOBILE ENGINE

: AN EXTENDED PART, CREST, OR MARKING ON OR NEAR THE HEAD OF AN
ANIMAL
THIS BROAD DEFINITION IS FAR FROM UNDERSTANDABLE.

THE POLITICAL, CULTURAL, AND ECONOMIC COMPREHENSION OF ASYLUM
ASSOCIATED THIS TERM WITH THAT OF A HOODLUM.

No longer a hoodlum, reduced to a thug;

still a tough-looking youth in need of a hug.
Knowledge of a condition can be bad or be good,
and should not limit the quality of a man's manhood.

For it is not up to man to recognize quality
but to introduce a solution that sets people free.

Exploring a term, often misunderstood
is to enrich just one life that still lives in the hood

———

JOURNAL EXPRESS 1

PONDER

There are many definitions given to the term, **hood**.

QUESTION #1:
What is the first thing you think of when you hear the term **hood**?
Why?

_____

_____

_____

_____

_____

_____

BABYHOOD

by Randall D.E. Beverly

MIRACULOUSLY FORMED AND SHAPED IN THE WOMB
AFTER NINE MONTHS OF GROWTH YOU RAN OUT OF ROOM
PREDESTINED TO BE LOVED AND NURTURED BY LIGHT
SECURED BY STRONG ARMS AND PROTECTED AT NIGHT

GROWTH IS INEVITABLE FROM CRADLE TO BED
FROM SOFT TO HARD FOOD YOU SOON WILL BE FED
SENT FROM ABOVE TO GIVE LIFE TO THE DEAD
ATTACHED WAS A NOTE SIMPLY STATED AND WELL SAID

WAS THE PURPOSE AND FUNCTION OF A BABY WHICH READ
"IF EVER SHOULD YOU QUESTION THE WORTH OF YOUR BIRTH
YOU ARE A GIFT SENT FROM HEAVEN TO PRESENT HEAVEN TO EARTH"

JOURNAL EXPRESS 2

PONDER

Babies can sense emotion. "By the time newborns are just a few months old, they can recognize the difference between a happy expression and a sad one.[1]"
Alison Gopnik, Ph.D

QUESTION #2:
Do you know your birth location and time?
How much did you weigh?
What have you ever been told about your birth?

TODDLERHOOD

by Randall D.E. Beverly

CURIOUS AND COURAGEOUS IN AN ATMOSPHERE EXPLORED
IN AWE OF NEW SURROUNDINGS TOO YOUNG TO BE BORED
HAS SKILLS TO CRAWL BUT CAN WALK NOW A BIT
ADULTS HAVE TO CHASE BUT STAY PHYSICALLY FIT

SUPERVISION MUST OFTEN PUT TO THE TEST
THIS STAGE OF EXISTENCE MAKES AN ADULT RESPECT REST
BUT WHEN ADULTS GET IT THEY ARE AWAKENED IT'S TRUE
AWAKENED TO THE PEACE IN WATCHING OVER OF YOU

STILL GIVEN A DESIRE TO TOUCH AND TO TASTE
LEARNING SMOOTH AND ROUGH TEXTURES WITH NO TIME TO WASTE
TO HEAR THE WORDS "NO NO" TO PROMOTE A RETREAT
MUST STILL TRY THE DIRT PIE THAT WAS MADE AS A TREAT

AND THEN THERE'S THE POTTY-THAT HUGE PORCELAIN HOLE
LEAVING DIAPERS BEHIND AS YOU PLAY IN THE BOWL
WHICH LEADS TO A BATH THAT IS GENTLE AND FAIR
AND LOVE FROM THOSE COMMITTED TO HANDLE WITH CARE

———

JOURNAL EXPRESS 3

PONDER

"Toddlers are instinctively attracted to shapes that resemble the human face.[1]"

Fiona McKim

QUESTION #3:
Has your family told you about how you were as a toddler?
Share one story below.

_____

_____

_____

_____

_____

CHILDHOOD

by Randall D.E. Beverly

PERFECTED WALKING STILL READY TO RUN
A LIST OF EXPECTATIONS FROM UNDER THE SUN
FROM HOME TO THE SCHOOLHOUSE, EXPOSED TO THE WORLD
IN IT BUT NOT OF IT YET STILL TAUGHT TO LOVE IT

LOVE THOSE TAUGHT TO LOVE AS WELL AS THOSE TAUGHT TO HATE
NEVER COMPROMISE THE PEARLS WHICH HOLD KEYS TO THE GATE
GIFTS TALENTS AND LOOKS WILL COME FROM THE PAST
AND PROVE TO BE GIFTS TO A FUTURE THAT CAST

INSIGHT BEYOND VISION IN EACH TOUGH DECISION
DECISIONS MORE IMPORTANT THAN THE OPINION OF OTHERS
MORE IMPORTANT THAN POWER POINTS AND PRIMARY COLORS
STAY TRUE TO THE FACTS AND THE PRICE THAT WAS PAID
FOR THE FACT STILL REMAINS THAT YOU ARE WONDERFULLY MADE

JOURNAL EXPRESS 4

PONDER

A strong parent-child bond in early childhood prepares children to better handle stress throughout life.[1]

QUESTION #4:
Do you like school? Why or why not?
What are some things you like to do for fun?

_____

_____

_____

_____

_____

_____

BROTHERHOOD

by Randall D.E. Beverly

OH BROTHER SURE GLAD TO FIND TRUTH IN YOU
FOR THE WORLD IS CONFUSED ABOUT HOW THEY SHOULD VIEW
THE SCRIPT THAT SAYS ONE SHOULD LOVE AT ALL TIMES
NOT SOMETIMES CONDITIONAL JUST TO EARN A FEW DIMES

OH BROTHER SURE GLAD YOU CHOSE TO STICK CLOSER
THAN OTHERS WHO TOSSED YOUR LOVE IN A TOASTER
TO BE BURNED AND USED FOR PERSONAL SATISFACTION
NOT KNOWING THE BREAD OF LIFE WOULD POP-UP AND TAKE ACTION

WARM TO THE TOUCH PLUS BUTTERED WITH SOUL
LOST A FEW CRUMBS YET STILL READY TO ROLL
IN A WORLD THAT LACKS VISION WISDOM UNDERSTANDING AND
KNOWLEDGE
BUT BELIEVES THAT SUCH THINGS CAN BE TAUGHT AT A COLLEGE

FOR MANY ARE CALLED BUT THE CHOSEN ARE FEW
BECAUSE SOME BUT NOT ALL ARE QUICK TO REFUSE
CLASS AND GOOD TASTE FOUND ONLY IN YOU

———

JOURNAL EXPRESS 5

PONDER

"Sometimes being a brother is even better than being a superhero,[1]"
Marc Brown

QUESTION #5:
Do you have brother(s)? How many?
Name one thing you like about your brother(s).
If you have no brother(s), do you have a close friend that is like a
brother? Explain.

_____

_____

_____

_____

_____

SISTERHOOD

by Randall D.E. Beverly

MY SISTER MY SISTER PLEASE KNOW YOUR WORTH
FOR YOUR COVENANT IS GOLDEN AND BRINGS MUCH TO THE EARTH
REPRESENTING BEAUTY AND PURITY THAT CRADLES CREATION
YOUR EXISTENCE DISTRACTS BUT ATTRACTS MANY NATIONS

FULL OF LUST PLUS A FEW LIES THAT ARE FILLED WITH DECEIT
DON'T BUY INTO A MINDSET THAT WILL REDUCE YOU TO MEAT
FOR YOUR GRACE IS UNTOUCHED AND YOUR SMELL REMAINS SWEET
DO NOT SOUR YOUR EXISTENCE BECAUSE OF YOUR FEET

FEET QUICK TO RUN FEET QUICK TO FIGHT
OVER A PRIDE THAT MISUSES YOUR PRECIOUS DELIGHT
YET STILL THERE REMAINS SISTERS MOTHERS AND GRANDMOTHERS
ALIKE

WHO WILL REACH JUST TO TEACH YOU TO RESPECT AND EXPECT MORE
FROM VALUE NEITHER PURCHASED NOR FOUND IN A STORE
YOU ARE MY SISTER AND YOU ARE LOVED NO NEED TO SAY MORE

JOURNAL EXPRESS 6

PONDER

"Sisters make the bad times good and the good times unforgettable.[1]"

QUESTION #6:
Do you have sister(s)? How many?
Name one thing you like about your sister(s).
If you have no sister(s), do you have a close friend that is like a sister?
Explain.

_____

_____

_____

_____

_____

KNIGHTHOOD

by Randall D.E. Beverly

BIOLOGICAL AND CHEMICAL TRANSITIONS APPLY
TO INFORM AND TRANSFORM UNINFORMED AS TO WHY
A NECESSARY OPPORTUNITY FROM BOYHOOD TO PUBERTY
LACKS LIBERTY TO MAKE SENSE, OF CHANGE, MADE IN THE BODY

BRACES AND ACNE ARE A REALITY NOW
BRACE YOURSELF FOR INSTRUCTIONS THAT COME WITH A VOW
TO GUIDE AND DIRECT THE LONG JOURNEY OF MEN
WHEN ELEMENTARY WAS POLISHED AND VALUED BACK THEN

BUT INTERMEDIATE DIVISION FINDS WAYS TO GET IN
TO CORRUPT A YOUNG MIND AS CLIQUES FORM AND BEGIN
BE CONSCIOUS AND BECOME GROUP-WISE BUT DON'T TRY TO FIT IN

FOR YOU WERE DESTINED FOR GREATNESS SINCE THE DAY OF YOUR
BIRTH
NEITHER CLASS STATUS NOR CLASS CLOWNS CAN DETERMINE YOUR
WORTH
SO HOLD FAST AS YOU GROW FAST AND CLING TO THE LIGHT
FOR THE LIGHT IS A KING WHO HAS DUBBED YOU A KNIGHT

———

JOURNAL EXPRESS 7

PONDER

Knights are known for their suit of armor, courage, and commitment to never give up when facing obstacles.

QUESTION #7:
What is a clique?
Have you ever been teased based on how you physically look, dress, where you live, or how much money you have? Explain.

_____

_____

_____

_____

_____

FALSEHOOD

by Randall D.E. Beverly

SOME LEARN TO SEND IT, WHILE OTHERS RECEIVE IT
WHETHER SENDER OR RECEIVER REFUSE TO BELIEVE IT
FOR IT IS DISGUISED AND PRESENTED AS ABSOLUTE TRUTH
BUT TRUTHFULLY IT'S A LIE A WELL-WRAPPED UNCOUTH

LIKE A DISEASE, ONE CAN CATCH IT, WITH NO SIGN OR SYMPTOMS
UNDETECTED STILL INFECTED ARE THE LIVES OF ITS VICTIMS
ON A MISSION TO DESTROY WITHOUT LEAVING A TRACE
AN ABSOLUTE TRUTH ALL PEOPLE MUST FACE

ITS FACEBOOK STOLE MY SPACE
AND MY SPACE, A SMALL PLACE
WHERE THERE STILL LIES ROOM TO EXAMINE IT
MAKE A CHOICE TO BELIEVE, SEND, OR EVEN RECEIVE IT

BUT IT IS ONLY BUILT TO LAST FOR A SEASON
AND PALES IN COMPARISON TO THE SPRING OF ONE REASON
TO PITCH IT OR DITCH IT WHEN TOLD AS A YOUTH-
ENDURE CHALLENGE AND CONTROVERSY THAT COMES WITH THE TRUTH

JOURNAL EXPRESS 8

PONDER

We lie loudest when we lie to ourselves.[1]
Eric Hoffer

QUESTION #8:
Have you ever told a lie?
Can you recall one lie you told that got you in trouble?
Have you ever told a lie that got you out of trouble? Explain.

_____

_____

_____

_____

_____

BACHELORHOOD

by Randall D.E. Beverly

SOME SAY "IT'S THE BEST TIME THAT I'VE EVER HAD"
FOR TIME PASSED AT THIS STAGE OFTEN COMES WITH A PAD,

A PAD FILLED WITH ROOMMATES YOU WILL NEVER FORGET
AND FORGET NOT THE TIME YOU MET A YOUNG BACHELORETTE

FOR THE BACHELORETTE YOU JUST MET IS NOW A CLOSE FRIEND
A CLOSE FRIEND THAT HELPS BACHELORHOOD COME TO AN END

JOURNAL EXPRESS 9

PONDER

A bachelor and bachelorette represents a man and woman who have never been married and will remain that way until they meet and decide to marry.

QUESTION #9:
What have you learned or been told about relationships between men and women?

_____

_____

_____

_____

_____

ADULTHOOD

by Randall D.E. Beverly

SOME ANTICIPATE ITS GREATNESS SOME APPROACH IT WITH FEAR
SOME CHOOSE TO DO NEITHER NOR EVEN QUESTION THE YEAR
THE YEAR ONE IS LINKED TO A MAJORITY RULE
THE YEAR ONE WILL GRADUATE OR DECIDE TO QUIT SCHOOL

THE YEAR ONE CAN VOTE AND JOIN THE MILITARY
THE YEAR ONE EMOTION CAN CAUSE ONE TO MARRY
THE YEAR ONE PREPARES FOR AN OPPORTUNITY
THE YEAR ONE CAN HEAR ONE EXCLAIM "I AM FREE!"

FREE AT LAST FREE AT LAST THANK GOD ALMIGHTY I AM FREE AT LAST
THE RULES THAT ONCE BOUND ME NOW LIVE IN THE PAST
I AM FREE TO MAKE CHOICES WITHOUT GUIDANCE OR PERMISSION
I AM FREE TO ENDURE THE CONSEQUENCES OF A GOOD OR BAD DECISION

I AM FREE TO GET A JOB TO EARN DOLLARS AND CENTS
I AM FREE TO LOSE FREEDOM IF I LACK COMMON SENSE

JOURNAL EXPRESS 10

PONDER

Adults were once children that now have bigger bodies and more responsibilities.

QUESTION #10:
Do you look forward to becoming an adult?
Name one adult you trust. Why?

_____

_____

_____

_____

_____

_____

LIVELIHOOD

by Randall D.E. Beverly

ASSOCIATED WITH STATUS AND MISUNDERSTOOD
A CRIME OFTEN COMMITTED TO ONE'S LIVELIHOOD
HOW BIG IS YOUR HOUSE OR WHAT KIND OF CAR DO YOU DRIVE
MERE QUESTIONS CANNOT DEFINE WHY YOU ARE ALIVE

DARE TO LOOK DEEPER THAN A PLANK OR SPECK
CHOOSE NOT TO FOLLOW THOSE SIMPLY CHASING A CHECK
BUT BE SURE TO CHECK PRIDE IF IT KNOCKS AT THE DOOR
FOR PRIDE TEACHES GREED AND GREED WILL HUNGER FOR MORE

MORE EXTERNAL POMPOSITY SERVED ON A PLATE
MORE INTERNAL INDIGESTION TO THE ONE WHO JUST ATE
A TASTE OF THE "GOOD LIFE" OFTEN MISUNDERSTOOD
THE CRIME OFTEN ACQUITTED POORLY DEFINED LIVELIHOOD

JOURNAL EXPRESS 11

PONDER

"Money is a good servant but a bad master.[1]*"*
Francis Bacon

QUESTION #11:
Have you ever been asked what you want to do for a living?
What was your response?
What kind of job would you like to have in the future? Why?

_____

_____

_____

_____

_____

WOMANHOOD

by Randall D.E. Beverly

THE WISE WILL RESPECT AND CHOOSE NOT TO NEGLECT IT
THE UNWISE WILL PLAY WISE AS THEY DESPISE AND REJECT IT
BE WISE TO NEVER MISUSE OR CHOOSE TO BRUTALIZE IT
BE CAREFUL TO TAKE CARE OF WHAT BLOSSOMS INSIDE IT

FOR WHAT BLOSSOMS INSIDE IT WILL ONE DAY DECIDE
TO RESPECT OR NEGLECT ONE CHOICE FILLED WITH PRIDE
A PRIDE THAT PROTECTS IT AND RESPECTS IT WILL LIVE
A PRIDE THAT DISRESPECTS AND NEGLECTS IT WILL GIVE

A SECOND THOUGHT TO ITS MISUSE AND CHOICE OF REJECTION
FROM A COURTROOM THAT SUPPORTS C.S.E.A COLLECTION
TO ADDRESS MISPLACED AFFECTION THAT COMES WITH A PRICE
BE WISE TO TAKE CARE OF WHAT CAN CARRY A LIFE

JOURNAL EXPRESS 12

PONDER

Without a woman there can be no man.

QUESTION #12:
According to you, what must a woman do to earn your respect?
Name one woman you trust? Why?

_____

_____

_____

_____

_____

_____

MANHOOD

by Randall D.E. Beverly

SOME LOVE TO LOVE IT
WHILE SOME LOVE TO HATE IT
YOUNG BOYS GROW TO MEN
CONGRATULATIONS YOU MADE IT

PAST THE TEST AND THE TRIALS THAT ARE SO UNDERRATED
STAY SCHOOLED BY AND FUELED BY THE ONES THAT HAVE HATED
CONNECTED TO POWER AND ENERGIZED BY LOVE
A TRUE SENSE OF CONNECTION TO WHAT IS ABOVE

YOUR OWN EXPECTATIONS THAT ARE BECOMING MORE CLEAR
TO MANY NATIONS THAT ARE GLAD AND SEEKING TO HEAR
YOU SHED LIGHT ON THIS GIFT WITHOUT QUESTION OR FEAR
FEAR NOT THE ONES THAT DO NOT WELCOME YOU HERE

JOURNAL EXPRESS 13

PONDER

Without a man there could be no woman.

QUESTION #13:

According to you, what must a man do to earn your respect?
Name one man that you trust? Why?

_____

_____

_____

_____

_____

_____

MOTHERHOOD

by Randall D.E. Beverly

NINE MONTHS OF SACRIFICE SUPPORTED BY CHOICE
A CRY DURING LABOR UPON HEARING YOUR VOICE
A DEDICATION TO FEED THE NURTURE YOU NEED
A DESIRE TO SEE YOU GROW TALL AND SUCCEED

A COMFORTING SMILE AND SENSITIVE TOUCH
WORDS THAT ENCOURAGE OFTEN NEEDED AS MUCH
AS AN ATTEMPT TO BRING PEACE THROUGH THE POWER OF SONG
A KNOWLEDGE TO KNOW WHEN SOMETHING IS WRONG

THIS WONDER AND STRENGTH DID NOT COME FROM THE DUST
BUT FROM A LOVE THAT IS PRICELESS THE 1ST LOVE YOU TRUST

JOURNAL EXPRESS 14

PONDER

The very first Mother's Day was celebrated in 1908.[1]

QUESTION #14:
What role has your mother played in your life?
Do you have a close relationship with your mother? Explain.
If you were not raised by your mother,
who would you consider a mother to you?

_____

_____

_____

_____

_____

FATHERHOOD

by Randall D.E. Beverly

A CHOICE TO BE PRESENT OR NON-EXISTENT
A CHILD WILL STILL LEARN IF YOUR ROLE IS CONSISTENT
CONSISTENT WITH A MINDSET COMMITTED AND TRUE
A MINDSET NOT BLINDED TO THE IMPORTANCE OF YOU

ENCOMPASSING A POWER THAT SETS PEOPLE FREE
ENTRUSTED TO BE ONE WHO REMAINS COMMITTED TO BE
A MAN WITH INTEGRITY THAT IS NEVER NEGLECTED
A MAN FAR FROM PERFECT, YET STILL WELL RESPECTED

A MAN THAT GIVES WATER TO ANY THAT THIRST
TO PURSUE WISDOM AND HONOR AND PUTS OTHERS FIRST
A MAN THAT IS STRONG NEVER TOO STRONG TO CRY
A MAN THAT SEEKS ANSWERS TO THE QUESTIONS OF WHY

A MAN THAT IS LOYAL TO HIS WIFE AND HIS KIDS
UNASHAMED AND SO THANKFUL FOR THE THINGS THAT YOU DID

JOURNAL EXPRESS 15

PONDER

The celebration of Father's Day officially began in 1910 by Sonora Dodd.[1]

QUESTION #15:
What role has your father played in your life?
Do you have a close relationship with your father? Explain.
If you were not raised by your father,
who would you consider a father to you?

_____

_____

_____

_____

_____

SELFHOOD

by Randall D.E. Beverly

SYMBOLIZES ROYALTY NOW MOCKED FOR THE MEANING
HISTORICAL RESPECT TO A SHAME SO DEMEANING
PICTORIAL PORTRAYALS OF CATHEDRALS AND WALLS
HOUSES MANY BLESSINGS WHILE EXPOSING THE FLAWS

OF A BLURRED INTERPRETATION OF AN IMPORTANT POSITION
EMBRACED BY A LIGHT AND YOUNG ROYAL WITH VISION
A VISION OF WISDOM COMPASSION AND STRENGTH
UNCONCERNED WITH THE MEASURE AND EVEN THE LENGTH

FOR THE LABEL RECEIVED REMAINS MORE THAN A NAME
A NAME THAT IS RESPECTED A NAME WITHOUT SHAME
THAT ENDURES PRESSURE AND HATE BUT NEVER GIVES IN
TO THE JUDGMENTS AND STONES CAST BY STONE-HEARTED MEN

JOURNAL EXPRESS 16

PONDER

The birth certificate and social security card only shows a portion of an individual's identity.

QUESTION #16:
What are three words you would use to describe yourself? Why?

_____

_____

_____

_____

_____

_____

NEIGHBORHOOD

by Randall D.E. Beverly

MOST OFTEN DEFINED BY THE LEVEL OF CRIME
GRADUAL INCREASE OR DECREASE IN VALUE AND TIME
STILL, TIMELESS MOTIVATION REMAINS WILLING AND ABLE
TO FIND WAYS TO TRANSCEND THE WEIGHT OF A LABEL

A LABEL THAT CHOOSES TO STAY IN A BOX
CHARACTERIZED BY A CITY A STREET OR A BLOCK
THAT COMES WITH A PRIDE THAT CLAIMS TO BE BEST
WHERE BULLETPROOF VESTS ARE STILL PUT TO THE TEST

A TEST THAT CONSUMES THE MIND OF MANKIND
NEED AN ANSWER TO WHY IT WAS ALL LEFT BEHIND
A MASK AND AN ORDER THAT IS READY TO LEARN
TO GIVE BACK TO A HOOD THAT WILL APPLAUD YOUR RETURN

JOURNAL EXPRESS 17

PONDER

Judgements get made at times based upon where an individual grew up.

QUESTION #17:
How would you describe your neighborhood?
Good or bad? Explain.
What, if anything, would you change about your neighborhood? Why?

_____

_____

_____

_____

_____

LIKELIHOOD

by Randall D.E. Beverly

IT IS HIGHLY UNLIKELY THAT EVERYONE WILL LIKE YOU
BUT AS LONG AS YOU LIKE YOU THEN IT IS LIKELY YOU KNEW
THAT GREATNESS IS NOT DEFINED BY THE MIND OF MANKIND
FOR YOUR WORTH WAS PREDESTINED SINCE THE BEGINNING OF TIME

BE SURE TO MAKE TIME TO EXPLORE WHAT IS NEW
NEW TALENTS AND GIFTS THAT DWELL WITHIN YOU
YOU WILL COME ACROSS MANY THAT SAY THEY DON'T CARE
BUT THEY DO SO STAY TRUE TO A DARE TO BE RARE

IN A WORLD OF OPINIONS AND MISPLACED PERSISTENCE
YOU WILL LIKELY BE WISE TO YOUR WELL-DEFINED EXISTENCE

JOURNAL EXPRESS 18

PONDER

Success, like beauty, is in the eye of the beholder.

QUESTION #18:
How do you define success?
Do you believe you will succeed in life?
Explain why or why not?

_____

_____

_____

_____

_____

_____

PARENTHOOD

by Randall D.E. Beverly

NEVER MEANT FOR A COWARD BUT PRESERVED FOR THE BOLD
A DISTINCT HONOR BESTOWED AMONGST THE YOUNG AND THE OLD

A TRUE CHALLENGE THAT GIVES BIRTH TO THE SEED THAT YOU SOW
A GENUINE OPPORTUNITY TO BUILD AND TO GROW
IN GOOD SOIL A YOUNG MIND NEEDING TO KNOW

THAT THE SEED THAT WAS PLANTED WAS MEANT TO PRODUCE
PRODUCTIVE MEMBERS OF SOCIETY IN A SOCIETY THAT VIEWS
THE GROWTH PLUS DEVELOPMENT AND DISPLAY OF A CHILD
REFLECTS AN INFLUENCE THAT HELPS THEM GROW TALL OR GROW WILD

PONDER

Parenting is not a job-but an opportunity to help children develop and grow their potential, self-esteem, and sense of purpose.

QUESTION #19:

On a scale of 1 (poor) to 10 (excellent), what rating would you give your parents/legal custodian?
What rating do you think they would give you? Explain.
What, if anything, would you change about your parents/legal custodian?

_____

_____

_____

_____

STATEHOOD

by Randall D.E. Beverly

IN THE STATE OF A UNION LET THE UNION ADDRESS
HOW THE STATE OF A UNION IS BECOMING A MESS
DIVIDED WE FALL BUT UNITED WE STAND
DISRUPTIONS AND RIOTS NOW COVER THIS LAND

MANY ADMINISTRATIONS AND UNFINISHED PLANS
TO BE MESSED WITH AND LEFT IN THE PALM OF THE HANDS
OF THE NEXT GENERATION THAT WILL DARE TO COMPLETE
THE UNFINISHED BUSINESS OF A STATE INCOMPLETE

INCOMPLETE OF A GOAL OR A GOAL THAT LACKS
TO HELP ONE STEP OVER AND NOT FALL THROUGH THE CRACKS
CRACKING THE CASE NO NEED FOR A SIGN
TO JUSTIFY A UNION LEAVING NO ONE BEHIND

JOURNAL EXPRESS 20

PONDER

Regardless of one's state of origin-the individual state of mind is most important!

QUESTION #20:
What state are you from? What is your state known for?
What, if anything, would you change about your state? Why?

_____

_____

_____

_____

_____

_____

SERVANTHOOD

by Randall D.E. Beverly

SERVICE WITH A SMILE CAN GO A LONG WAY
A WAY THAT CAN CAUSE A GOOD SERVANT TO STAY
MOTIVATED AND INSPIRED AT WORK OR AT PLAY
CAN LEAD TO PROMOTION AND INCREASE IN PAY

PAY ATTENTION TO THOSE THAT HAVE A BAD DAY
BAD DAYS CAN CAUSE ONE TO PUSH YOU AWAY
AWAY ONE MAY PUSH BUT PUSH THROUGH NO DELAY
WITH AN ATTITUDE OF GRATITUDE AND SOMETHING TO SAY

ABOUT YOUR SERVICE THAT WILL BE KNOWN AND EMBRACED BY A
NATION
THANKFUL YOU WERE SERVED TO SERVE THE NEXT GENERATION

JOURNAL EXPRESS 21

PONDER

Be careful to be the service you want to receive.

QUESTION #21:
Have you ever served someone? How was your service received?
Have you ever received bad service? How did it make you feel?
In what way(s) do you think you can serve your community?

_____

_____

_____

_____

_____

DEAR READER

Thank you for the time, energy, and resources that you have invested in navigating through the pages of this journal. I hope you enjoyed the journey and I look forward to our next encounter. Until we meet again, make it a point to start and finish each day with purpose on purpose with a smile. Know that you were destined for greatness since before the day of your birth, and always be...

ENCOURAGED *to be the best version of yourself.*

MOTIVATED *to build and maintain positive relationships.*

INSPIRED *to promote positive change in an ever-changing world.*

Sincerely/Respectfully Yours,

Randall D. E. Beverly

REFERENCES

JOURNAL EXPRESS 2

1. 6 Things You May Not Know Your Baby Can Do, article by Leslie Garisto Pfaff (parents.com).

JOURNAL EXPRESS 3

1. 10 of the most fascinating toddler facts, article by Fiona McKim (juniormagazine.co.uk)

JOURNAL EXPRESS 4

1. Fast Facts about Children's Brain Development, compiled by the Marisco Institute for Early Learning and Literacy-University of Denver, Morgridge College of Education (milwaukee.extension.wis.edu).

JOURNAL EXPRESS 5

1. The Greatest Brother Quotes and Sibling Sayings-2017-2020. Quote Ambition. (quoteambition.com).

JOURNAL EXPRESS 6

1. The Top 100 Sister Quotes and Funny Sayings with Images-2017-2020. Quote Ambition. (quoteambition.com).

JOURNAL EXPRESS 8

1. Brainy Quote (brainyquote.com)

JOURNAL EXPRESS 11

1. Francis Bacon-publicquotes.com

JOURNAL EXPRESS 14

1. 20 Mother's Day Facts to Share with you Mom-article by Leah Silverman (May 6, 2020) townandcountrymag.com

JOURNAL EXPRESS 15

1. Media & Culture-Father's Day History: 9 Interesting Facts You May Not Know About The Holiday And Its Origins-article by Julia Glum on 6/20/15 at 8:19pm (ibtimes.com).

ABOUT THE AUTHOR

Randall D.E. Beverly is a native of Chillicothe, Ohio.

He holds a Bachelor of Arts degree in English/Humanities from Shawnee State University. He also holds a Master of Social Sciences degree from Ohio University.

He has experience teaching at the collegiate level and created the Sandra J. Cousins Memorial Scholarship in honor of his mother to help high school seniors pursue a post-secondary education.